ABOUT THE AUTHOR

Marko Kloos is the author of two military science fiction series: The Palladium Wars, which includes *Aftershocks* and *Ballistic*, and the Frontlines series, which includes, most recently, *Points of Impact*. Born in Germany and raised in and around the city of Münster, Marko was previously a soldier, bookseller, freight dockworker, and corporate IT administrator before deciding that he wasn't cut out for anything except making stuff up for fun and profit. A member of George R. R. Martin's Wild Cards consortium, Marko writes primarily science fiction and fantasy—his first genre loves ever since his youth, when he spent his allowance on German SF pulp serials. He likes bookstores, kind people, October in New England, fountain pens, and wristwatches. Marko resides at Castle Frostbite in New Hampshire with his wife, two children, and roving pack of voracious dachshunds. For more information visit www.markokloos.com.

Passacaglia
on an Old English Tune

Viola

Rebecca Clarke

Viola

a tempo, ma poco a poco allargando

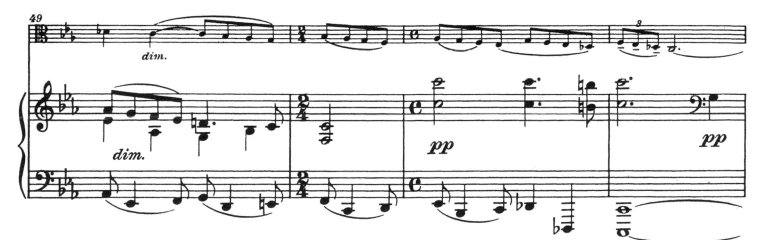

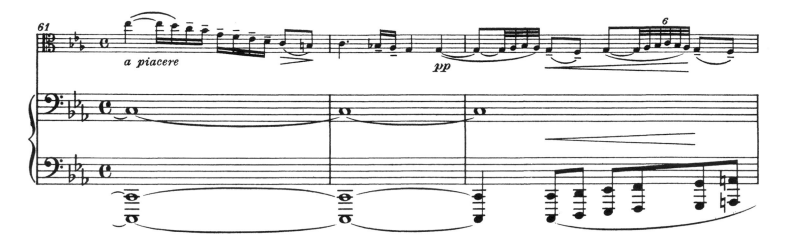

U.S. $9.99

ISBN 978-0-634-00565-7

0 73999 83591 5

HL50483591

G. SCHIRMER, *Inc.*

DISTRIBUTED BY
HAL•LEONARD®

ISBN-13: 978-0-634-00565-7

Distributed By

HAL LEONARD

50483591

9 780634 005657